Her Essential Quotations

Delaplaine Essential Quotations
Editor - Andrew Delaplaine
Illustrator - Renee Delaplaine

Gramercy Park Press
New York – London - Paris

gppress@gmail.com

Life passes into pages if it passes into anything.

■ *James Salter*

In a theater you have that many more seats, so that many more people, and they are feeding you, telling you how far you can go or what you can do.

And I hate autobiographies, I don't know why.

Life is filled with a lot of stuff, you know. There is never a dull moment.

Every time you perform you learn a little bit more.

If you would have told me ten years ago I'd be doing this and being received like I am now, I'd say you're crazy.

I can't say it's autobiographical, but I do tell a number of anecdotes that I think are amusing.

But I've been doing it most of my adult life, and I like the idea of a one woman show, because it's something I can do when I want to, and not to it when I don't want to do it.

In the show I actually talk a lot about how TV has changed.

Now this goes to the grave with you - I hate cheesecake!

No, no. I was never that involved in anything political actually.

For us it was really the same, because we did the show in front of a live audience, it was like being on stage.

I really cut my teeth on off-off-off Broadway shows.

But I've been doing it most of my adult life, and I like the idea of a one woman show, because it's something I can do when I want to, and not to it when I don't want to do it.

I've been blessed with both shows, with that and with Maude, working with terrific writers and directors.

That's another reason that I don't want to do any more series. It really took up more time than I should have allotted to it.

At least I'm not playing other people for a change. It's a very odd place to be... I feel I'm an actress who sings a bit.

I guess having two kids who are bright and articulate and have great humor and are decent.

I don't know, I didn't know I was that vibrant, I just love being alive, and I love people, and I find something wonderful everyday.

I can't imagine working without and audience.

Except for one thing, I no longer do benefits for research, I do benefits to make sure the people who are infected are taken care of are treated, and fed and housed, and their lives made a little easier.

So what does it all mean? You become a popular TV personality. Fifteen million viewers weekly. Top ratings.

I'm here now in Chicago doing my own show, and I think Golden Girls is shown three hours a day here, and everybody loves it.

It's so rewarding when you hear the audience respond.

I think the mother-daughter between Estelle and me was one made in comedy heaven.

It's a very small operation, there are five of us traveling, and I like working with different audiences, seeing how different it is from one night to the next.

I watch a lot of news shows and I love Nick at Night, and the Comedy Channel.

You see I feel we did the best work we could possibly do, I don't think the writing could be any better, so why go back to it?

When you are working with someone it's like family, you are together every day.

But that's one of the nice things about doing a stage show, if something doesn't work out, you have the luxury of working on it over time.

Some people say I'm only happy when I'm working, or not working, I'm happy whether I'm working or not, my animals, my kids, anything.

Down in Florida it was an older audience, and it was interesting to see how they responded to things compared to other audiences, it's been very interesting.

But I did like the fact that we did a lot of good in presenting problems that had not been tackled before on television.

I did a thing on “Malcolm in the Middle” which I loved.

I'd never even been to Wrigley Field. I never even enjoyed baseball that much, but I loved being there, the crowd was lovely, and they all sang with me!

Making lasting shelters for animals in our estate plans is perhaps the single most important thing we can do to ensure animals have the strongest possible voice for their protection.

It's so rewarding when you hear the audience respond

For us it was really the same, because we did the show in front of a live audience, it was like being on stage.

I watch a lot of news shows and I love Nick at Night, and the Comedy Channel.

PETA has a proven track record of success. Each victory PETA wins for the animals is a stepping stone upon which we build a more compassionate world for all beings - and we will never give up our fight until all animals are treated with respect and kindness.

I believe that you're here on Earth for a short time, and while you're here, you shouldn't forget it.

I don't think there was ever an embarrassment, there was such love going back and forth between the audience and us, that nothing was embarrassing.

You know, I spend most of my life turning things down. There's a lot of crap out there.

I suddenly realized that comedy, for me, was just being honest, and playing it for real. I've seen so many wonderful actors who turn into creatures from another planet when they're told they are supposed to be playing comedy.

I'm not playing a role. I'm being myself, whatever the hell that is.

I... was not too happy to suddenly take on this public role thrust upon me. They just assumed I was the Joan of Arc of the women's movement. And I wasn't at all. It put a lot of unnecessary pressure on me.

I've seen so many excellent actors - excellent actors - who, the minute they're told they're in a comedy, turn into God knows what - creatures from another planet! I mean they just... the voice changes, they don't look the same, it's like - it has no similarity to any living human being, do you know what I mean? Or don't you? And I'm not talking about Sylvester Stallone... but there's a good example. You know what I mean? It comes down to what I said at the beginning of this: belief, truth... It's truth.

I'm very, very involved in charities involving youth.

I really feel all my adult life has been spent in that little black box. If a wonderful part on TV came I along I would do it. But I don't want to do a recurring role. It would just be my luck that the thing would be successful. I'm old enough now and also secure enough financially that I really only want to do what I want to do.

I love cooking, I love reading, I love anything that doesn't take too much exercise!

There was so much more we wanted to cover on the show, but since I couldn't get the network censors to budge, I decided to leave the show.

I've lost quite a bit of weight since I did Maude, but I don't see myself looking better, I think I look older. Because I am!

And of course Mae West when I was very, very young, I thought she was the end.
Influences on her

I think I always sang, I always used to listen to old Bessie Smith records, and Kate Smith. And Billie Holiday. Before television when there was radio.

Unfortunately opening night in Minneapolis I fell off the stage.

Except I really wanted to be a small little blonde musical type in the movies. I wanted to be a starlet.

The only one I wanted to do that I didn't was Gypsy, but by the time they got around to asking me, everybody in the world had played it, so I thought now is not the time.

But of course, it's very nice to have women realize that women our age can be attractive and well groomed and wear fabulous clothes and earrings, and have a sex life.

I have two enormous Dobermans, they couldn't possibly fly with me.

After being in the business for such a long time, I've done everything but rodeo and porno.

Keep fighting for animals by making compassionate, cruelty-free choices every day and encouraging those around you to do the same.

I don't think there was ever an embarrassment, there was such love going back and forth between the audience and us, that nothing was embarrassing.

My dream was to become a very small blonde movie star like Ida Lupino and those other women I saw up there on the screen during the Depression.

In sitcoms, the women are so beautiful, understanding and well-bred. They have humor, but sort of display it with a twinkle of the eye and not a guffaw. But there's no juice in that for me.

All this time I've just wanted to be blonde, beautiful and 5 feet 2 inches tall.

You know, the real name of this show is "Vera". The only reason they changed the name was because Jerry [lyricist Jerry Herman] couldn't think of a rhyme for it. Stephen Sondheim could have.
On playing Vera Charles in "Mame"

Our mother-daughter relationship was one of the greatest comic duos ever, and I will miss her.
When Estelle Getty died in 2008

Let's face it, nobody ever asked me to play Juliet.

There comes a morning when you wake up and realize you're not Barbra Streisand. If a woman my age is still fighting for roles, it can only mean there's something missing from her personal life.

No, no, don't call me Ms. I don't go along with this liberation thing. Liberation from what?

I don't think they realized how completely vulnerable I am. Matter of fact, I may start crying right now; if you let me.

I stayed with it for 7 years. I think, definitely, I made the right decision, cause we had highs that we couldn't top.
When "The Golden Girls" was canceled

I have had six full years. It's been glorious, I've loved every minute of it. But it has been six years and I think it's time to leave.
When "Maude" was canceled

Norman has had an idea some time ago in which Maude becomes a congresswoman and moves to Washington. Norman said if you go on for another year, we'll do it in Washington with a new cast. And if you don't, it's a hell of a way to end the show.

If I could only repeal the law of gravity.
As she aged

I really feel that I'm an exposed nerve... I don't know how else to say it, but I am. I'm moved by everything.

[In 1976]: Other than that it was a fun show to do. But I'll tell you one thing. That's the first and last time you'll see me on a horse - white or any color. The first person to suggest I do a Matt Dillon impression is not going to walk without pain for a week!

This show was every bit as tough as the analysis' show, but at least I wasn't out there all alone so that made it almost bearable. Of course the fact that we all had the flu and none of us had had time for Christmas shopping didn't make it easier.
After becoming famous in her 50s as Maude Findlay

I've been a Democrat my whole life. That's what makes Maude and Dorothy so believable, we have the same viewpoints on how our country should be handled.

I like to be myself and rest.
Why she spent so much time alone as she got older

She had all her marbles, she was in great shape, but she was almost totally deaf and almost totally blind, and really just wanted out. It was really something, Anyway, you do what you have to do. So. Why are all these people suffering from AIDS? You think—do it. Don't prolong it. I'm sure I don't feel any different from anybody else about that... I would rather they died than see the terrible ravages of this horrendous disease.

Why she was so caring about the elderly, after her mother committed suicide

Why, I never heard of that! My name? You mean, my real name? Are you serious? It's the first I've heard of that. The first I've heard of that! What does that mean? No one ever consulted me. No, in the movie that I made with Jason Alexander called "For Better or Worse", I absolutely refused screen credit,

because I felt the part wasn't that important, and I didn't feel that I did that great a job in it. But I don't remember a pseudonym.
Asked if she was ever credited as 'Jane Ross'.

A FEW QUOTES FROM HER SHOWS

That are my personal favorites

Dorothy: You'll have to excuse my mother; she suffered a slight stroke a few years ago, which rendered her totally annoying.

Blanche: Dorothy, when I'm feeling low self-esteem, I do a little exercise. I say my name and then three positive things about myself. I'm Blanche Devereaux.

I'm beautiful, men find me desirable, and people want to be my friend. Dorothy, now you try it.
Dorothy: Ah, I don't want to.
Blanche: Come on. Please.
Dorothy: Okay. I'm Dorothy Zbornak, I'm beautiful, men find me desirable and people want to be my friend.
Blanche: Oh no, I think I confused you there. I meant three things that apply to you. Like, I'm Dorothy Zbornak, I'm a good speller, and uh... I'm very prompt, and umm... Well, there's no law that says there have to be three good things.
Dorothy: Um... I just thought of a third one: she can break a friend's neck like a twig.

Blanche: With Ernie? With Ernie?! Rose, I'm so happy for you!
Dorothy: Blanche, calm down! It was a roll in the hay, not a walk on the moon!

Rose tells about the date she had with Ernie, who had been impotent till he slept with Rose

Rose [about Miles]: He makes me feel foolish. I don't even feel comfortable telling him St. Olaf stories.
Dorothy: I want to know exactly what he said to make you feel that way.

Rose: Blanche, you should make us eat dirt, make us grovel, give us the silent treatment...
Dorothy: Rose, if you give us the silent treatment, I will eat dirt.
Dorothy and Rose are apologizing to Blanche after a fight

Sophia: Dorothy, why don't we bond?
Dorothy: We're from before bonding and quality time.

Rose: Dorothy, a man called for you while you were out.
Sophia: Finally. Now we can break out that bottle of champagne we've been saving.
Dorothy: Ma-a...
Sophia: Come on, Dorothy, we might not get another chance.
Dorothy: Oh sure we will. We can just serve it at... the wake.

Blanche: Oh Dorothy, I just talked to somebody back home, and they are doing the most horrible thing! They are tearing down the most important building in Blanche Devereaux's family history.

Dorothy: Oh my God, they're tearing down Mattress World.
Blanche: Even worse than that. They are tearing down the place where I spent my happiest moments as a child.
Dorothy: Oh I'm sorry, Blanche. They're tearing down Boys Town.

Dorothy: Oh come on, Ma, that's superstitious nonsense. You know, step on a crack, break your mother's back, it doesn't work. — I know.

Rose: Why are you both wearing black? Did you just get back from a funeral?
Dorothy: No Rose, we were singing back-up for Johnny Cash.

Blanche: Now, only women in there twenties and thirties have babies, whatever is a woman in her forties to do?
Dorothy: I don't know, why don't we find one and ask?

Dorothy [to Rose]: So you're five years older, so am I, so is Blanche. Alright, so you have a few more wrinkles, so do I, so does Blanche. Okay, so you're a little thicker around the middle, so is Blanche.

Dorothy: I have a date.
Blanche: With a man?
Dorothy: No, Blanche, with a venus fly trap!

Dorothy: Rose, do you know off-hand if nine-one-one is the number to call for a strait jacket?
Rose: Dorothy, I can explain...
Dorothy: I know you can, that's the scary part!
Rose is using her nose to play a tune on a tiny piano & Dorothy comes in

Dorothy [to Sophia]: You are a furry gnome and we feed you too much!

Dorothy: Yes Rose, you are the smartest person in the world... Burger World!

Dorothy: The doctor says I have to have surgery.

Rose: Surgery, what for?
Dorothy: For KICKS, Rose!

Other Books by the Same Author

Andrew Delaplaine has written in widely varied fields: screenplays, novels (adult and juvenile), travel writing, journalism. His books are available in quality bookstores as well as all online retailers.

JACK HOUSTON ST. CLAIR POLITICAL THRILLERS

On Election night, as China and Russia mass soldiers on their common border in preparation for war, there's a tie in the Electoral College that forces the decision for President into the House of Representatives as mandated by the Constitution.

The incumbent Republican President, working through his Aide for Congressional Liaison, uses the Keystone File, which contains dirt on every member of Congress, to blackmail members into supporting the Republican candidate.

The action runs from Election Night in November to Inauguration Day on January 20.

Jack Houston St. Clair runs a small detective agency in Miami. His father is Florida Governor Sam Houston St. Clair, the Republican candidate. While he tries to help his dad win the election, Jack also gets hired to follow up on some suspicious wire transfers involving drug smugglers, leading him to a sunken narco-sub off Key West that has $65 million in cash in its hull.

THE ADVENTURES OF SHERLOCK HOLMES IV

In this series, the original Sherlock Holmes's great-great-great grandson solves crimes and mysteries in the present day, working out of the boutique hotel he owns on South Beach.

THE BORNHOLM DIAMOND

A mysterious Swedish nobleman requests a meeting to discuss a matter of such serious importance that it may threaten the line of succession in one of the oldest royal houses in Europe.

THE RED-HAIRED MAN

A man with a shock of red hair calls on Sherlock Holmes to solve the mystery of the Red-haired League.

THE CLEVER ONE

A former nun who, while still very devout, has renounced her vows so that she could "find a life, and possibly love, in the real world." She comes to Holmes in hopes that he can find out what happened to the man who promised to marry her, but mysteriously disappeared moments before their wedding.

THE COPPER BEECHES

A nanny reaches out to Sherlock Holmes seeking his advice on whether she should take a new position when her prospective employer has demanded that she cut her hair as part of the job.

THE MAN WITH THE TWISTED LIP

In what seems to be the case of a missing person, Sherlock Holmes navigates his way through a maze of perplexing clues that leads him through a sinister world to a surprising conclusion

THE DEVIL'S FOOT

Holmes's doctor orders him to take a short holiday in Key West, and while there, Holmes is called on to look into a case in which three people involved in a Santería ritual died with no explanation.

THE BOSCOMBE VALLEY MYSTERY

Sherlock Holmes and Watson are called to a remote area of Florida overlooking Lake Okeechobee to investigate a murder where all the evidence points to the victim's son as the killer. Holmes, however, is not so sure.

THE SIX NAPOLEONS

Inspector Lestrade calls on Holmes to help him figure out why a madman would go around Miami breaking into homes and businesses to destroy cheap busts of the French Emperor. It all seems very insignificant to Holmes—until, of course, a murder occurs.

Made in the USA
Middletown, DE
16 November 2017